Animal Doctors

by Darleen Ramos

 HOUGHTON MIFFLIN   BOSTON

PHOTOGRAPHY CREDITS: Cover © Blend Images/Jupiter Images; tp, 3 (tl) © age fotostock/SuperStock; 3 (tr) © Photodisc/SuperStock; 3 (bl) © Stockbyte/SuperStock; 3 (br) © Getty Images; 4 © Jupiter Images/Thinkstock/Alamy; 5 © Digital Vision Ltd./SuperStock; 6 © Richard Hutchings/Corbis; 7 © Blend Images/Jupiter Images; 8 © The Emporia Gazette/David Doemland/Associated Press; 9 © Source Agency image100/age fotostock; 11 © Digital Vision Ltd./SuperStock; 12 © Jeff Moore/Topham/The Image Works; 13 © Bob Krist/CORBIS; 14 © Cindy Charles/PhotoEdit.

Printed in China

ISBN-13: 978-0-547-02181-2
ISBN-10: 0-547-02181-X

5 6 7 8 9 0940 15 14 13 12 11 10

It's time to take your dog for a walk. You grab the leash and are surprised that he doesn't come running. He loves walks! You find the dog curled up on his bed. His eyes are open, but he doesn't seem to have any energy. He hasn't touched his food. You tell your mom, and she says the dog needs to see the doctor.

Veterinarians, or "vets" for short, are animal doctors. They help sick or hurt animals and also give advice to pet owners. Let's take a closer look to see what a vet's day is like.

Pets as Patients

On some days, vets get to play with healthy puppies and kittens. Most days, though, vets see sick animals—cats, dogs, rabbits, birds, and even ferrets. Like human patients, most pets have appointments on certain days and times. Other animals have emergencies. No two days are alike. Vets have exciting jobs.

Vets see all kinds of animals.

Many vets have separate waiting areas for dogs and cats.

Vets begin taking appointments early in the morning. Most appointments last 15 to 20 minutes. Some animals only need quick yearly exams and shots. Others need more time because they are sick. The vet must diagnose the problem and treat it.

Vets have to be good listeners. They listen to a pet's owner to find out the animal's symptoms. Then they ask a lot of questions about the animal's habits and behaviors. They also ask about how the owner takes care of the pet. A vet might ask what a sick animal has eaten or when it last drank water.

Even iguanas get sick!

After talking to the owner, vets look to the pet for answers. Good vets use their senses to examine the animal from nose to tail. A vet uses her eyes to see a wound or an infection. Her hands feel for any bumps or broken bones.

A vet examines the animal's body.

Vets use their ears, too. They listen for wheezing or gurgling noises. A pet might whimper or growl if it is in pain. Finally, vets rely on their noses. They might notice strange or sour smells. "Talking" to the animals takes a lot of practice.

Taking care of animals requires a lot of skill and patience.

Vets also take other steps to diagnose a sick animal. For example, they run tests. A vet might order a blood test or an X-ray. These tests help vets figure out what is wrong with the animal. After the vet learns what is wrong, he or she can choose the right medicine.

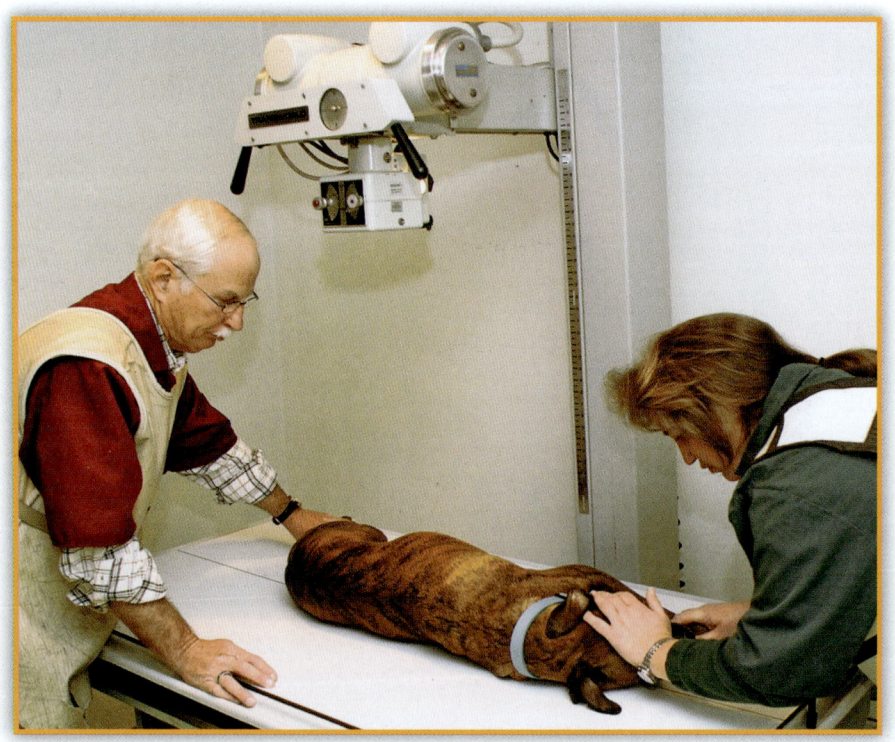

Vets perform tests on sick animals.

Surgery

Sometimes a vet <mark>performs</mark> surgery on an animal. They must prepare the animals. First, some hair is shaved and the pet is put to sleep so it doesn't feel pain. The vet will make a cut in the shaved area. Later, when the cut has healed, the hair will grow back. After surgery, some pets must spend the night at the clinic.

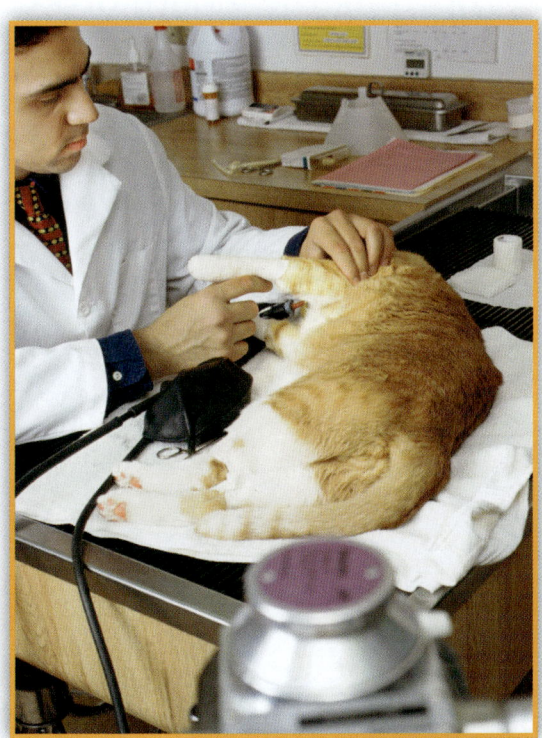

A surgeon can save a pet's life.

Just like people, pets need yearly checkups. All pets should get shots to prevent illness and disease. The vet weighs the animal and checks its eyes, ears, nose, and heart. The vet makes sure the animal is eating the right food and getting enough exercise. The vet even has to look inside the animal's mouth. Imagine opening the mouth of a Great Dane!

Some pets don't mind all this poking and prodding. Others do. "My dog is afraid of the vet, just like I'm afraid of the dentist!" confesses a pet owner.

Emergencies

Dogs and cats are always getting into trouble. They swallow all sorts of objects, such as needles, rubber bands, and golf balls. Sometimes they run around too much when it's hot outside and get heatstroke. Other times, they disobey their owners and run into the street, where they can get hurt.

Animals are often up to something!

Animal emergencies do not require appointments. In these cases, a vet checks the injured pet right away. If the animal has a broken leg or is bleeding heavily, surgery might be needed right away. Sometimes, a vet might find foster families to take care of recovering pets until permanent homes are found for them.

An animal might need a cast if it breaks its leg.

If you love animals, you might want to become a vet. You will need to study biology and chemistry and graduate from, or finish, veterinary school.

A vet's hours are long. They often have to work on weekends. However, nothing feels better than saving an animal's life and making people happy.

Veterinary School means four more years of studying after college.

Glossary

blood test a way to find illness or disease by checking what is in blood

clinic a place where patients are treated

diagnose to figure out a patient's disease or illness

surgery an operation on a patient

symptoms signs of an illness or disease

Rabbits need checkups, too!

Responding

✔ **TARGET SKILL** **Sequence of Events** What are some of the events that take place when a sick pet first comes to the vet's office? Copy and add more events to the chart below.

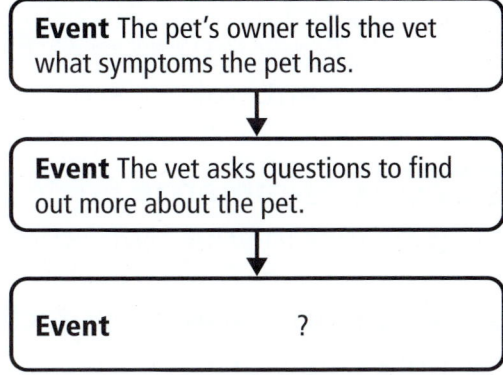

Event The pet's owner tells the vet what symptoms the pet has.

↓

Event The vet asks questions to find out more about the pet.

↓

Event ?

Write About It

Text to World Write a letter to a local vet. Include details that you learned about a vet's day from the book. Then ask the vet at least two questions.

ceremony	graduate
confesses	patiently
confidence	performs
disobey	reward
foster	symbol

✓ **TARGET SKILL** **Sequence of Events** Examine the time order in which events take place.

✓ **TARGET STRATEGY** **Summarize** Briefly tell the important parts of text in your own words.

GENRE **Narrative Nonfiction** gives factual information by telling a true story.